A Sense of Estonia

Fred Jüssi

Text and photos Fred Jüssi ©
Translated by Riina Kindlam
Design and layout Külli Kuusik
Editor Katrin Streimann

AS Ajakirjade Kirjastus, 2006
All rights reserved

Printed at Tallinna Raamatutrükikoda
ISBN 9949-427-02-9

Here, dear reader, is a small sampling of stories about Estonia.

They are experiences which have accumulated over time, just as water gathers in an old well. They are very important to me, since when I return to them, it's like going to the well, pail in hand – always refreshing and therapeutic.

I have quenched my thirst in mountain streams and tundra lakes, but nowhere have I drunk water as invigorating as that found in my old home well.

Fred Jüssi

DIRECTION

It's so hard to talk about nothing. I'd like to, but don't know how. Evening is evening, boulders are boulders, ice is ice and silence is silence. That's it. Naturally there are foxes' tracks, but the fox itself is nowhere to be seen. The cold begins to bite your face and fingertips. It's interesting that my experience of nothingness from a year ago has made such a place for itself deep inside my soul; this air and evening light. But there was a certain sound that one time: the shattering of ice. The wind on the open sea began to push the thin ice and it piled up onto the rocks, breaking into shimmering rosy pieces. Everything was very different from the summer. It's not even possible to reach Vaika Island via the Vilsandi lighthouse each winter, since ice conditions vary and you must be careful with possible open water if you're a stranger here.

It's a beautiful scene. A little unnerving as well. I recall having read a book as a boy entitled "Öös ja jääs" (In the Night and Frozen). It was about polar researchers, but I no longer remember exactly who or what, only the title. And so here it is, that frozen sea in the twilight. The final frontier, beyond which there is no more access. Somewhere, off to the west, are the seals and migratory birds, but this is your limit and you can't go any further. The night grows close. I listen to the shattering ice and wonder what would happen if I too, did not return. As if there are few, who have been lost to the night and the ice.

I turn to go and step towards the blinking of the Vilsandi lighthouse, feeling the breath of the ice fields on the back of my neck. Going back to my loved ones. Back to my joys and sorrows. To contemplate the idea of the pointlessness of the world. The lighthouse shows me the way.

SNOWSQUALL

The snow had been sparkling in the radiant sun all day, but in the evening, the western sky showed signs of an impending storm. And in the middle of the night the snowstorm began. The wind moaned in the stovepipe, rattled the damper and shook the window frames. Someone was clattering on the roof. Somebody was shuffling in the attic. Someone was wheezing on the porch. The house creaked and groaned. By morning the house was "cold like a wolf's barn", as my mother used to say on bitterly cold winter mornings and the wind kept gaining strength.

After a lengthy gathering of willpower, I arose from bed, went to the window and pushed aside the curtain. I could see that almost nothing could be seen. Only the tips of fence posts and the corner of the woodshed were visible, everything else was one great rage of snow.

After a cup of coffee, I pulled on my high boots and fur coat, stuffed my camera under my jacket and went outside. Oh, what a blizzard, awakening forgotten times and longings of old! On the infrequent occasions I find myself in such a squall, a piece by Juhani Aho comes to mind.

"Winter, when you drifted snow again… When you blew snow onto the roads again, along which all the world's travelling men ride with chimes and sleighbells, calling and shouting, and drift snow onto the edge of the road which they trample, trying to ride past each other; and into the highway's ditches into which they roll in a reeling race and the white banks they stomp on, as they fly head over heels…

You squalled onto the village roads, which meander muddily from farm to farm and along which all the people march as slaves, for no one dares straighten out what was once walked crooked by another; and onto farm roads and into backyards, where life has placed its enduring seal, which cannot be removed by crowbar or steel spade. /…/

You would snow people and beasts into their caves and barricade the doors from outside, so for five long days, they wouldn't dare emerge… Then I would see that even humans have a superior, that the most powerful has an equal /…/. I could watch as the world's races come to a halt, no one can get ahead of the other, instead all the sledges drag on in a long procession, as friends. /…/ If you would drift snow again for this reason, would hide all the old paths and force people to open up new roads for themselves."

/Juhani Aho "Laastud" (Shavings), The First Bundle, 1927. Translated from Finnish by Johannes Aavik/

I wade amongst the junipers, stumble along a stone fence, enveloped by the whining gale. I squint and try to take a picture. I lose my way. There are drifts everywhere. Suddenly everything looks totally different. It's as if it wasn't the same old familiar piece of land, as if it wasn't a quick journey of necessity to this Estonian backcountry, but rather a moment from another, inner time and world; a moment when all races come to a halt and force you to once again open new inroads for yourself – finally…

BLACKBIRD

The blackbird is a relatively common bird, but I don't dare say "we all know the blackbird". When I played bird songs to people at a rural gathering years ago, I discovered that of the 120 people in the hall, only one recognized the blackbird's song. The situation doesn't seem to get any better when the bird is identified by its appearance. It continues to be mistaken for the starling, since they're both black and their beaks are yellow in spring. And they both skip around on the ground and both know how to sing and both take off in flight if you get too close, but yet they don't interact in the spring, fall or winter. Their lifestyles are simply too different.

When speaking of the blackbird, we should've started with their song. They are one of the first to sing in the spring, on the heels of the tit. In any case, it isn't possible to confuse the pondering flutist in black with anyone else when he opens his beak in a park tree or on a TV antenna for the first spring serenade. The blackbird is a migratory bird, but during the last century and a half it has changed its habits and become a regular wintering bird as well, especially in cities and smaller communities. Ten or more years ago, a crowd of people stood on a path in Tallinn's Estonia Park and listened to a blackbird's New Year's Eve solo by the light of the streetlamps, which the bird devotedly performed to the fullest. Someone thought the singer had "gone slightly mad" and perhaps we shouldn't be surprised if he had.

Blackbirds don't otherwise sing in winter, they do so starting in late March, but they do screech, when something or someone bothers them. They begin courting locally in March, when the migrating blackbirds are also back home. They fuss with nest building in April, first fighting over women and real estate, and they totally forget themselves during these fights. I once watched in amazement how a ball of feathers, made up of two battling blackbirds, rolled through my legs as I was standing on the park lawn in Kärdla. *Well, come on now!* is what I wanted to call out, but when I turned around to face the gladiators, they were already gone.

You must try to stay alive in January. This is much easier in the city, surrounded by big consumers like humans, than in the country or forest. If something edible is not found on a birdfeeder, then by a garbage can most definitely. There aren't enough rowanberries each year to feed everyone during the long winter months. Our climate is harsh. It's a good year if half of the blackbirds survive; in Britain four out of ten are thought to perish.

Blackbirds are faithful to region. They may sometimes raise two or three broods in the same nest, but this need not always be with the same mate. So that you may be well informed to make your decision, dear readers, as to whether nature is our only example to follow, or not. And another important fact about the blackbird: the *point* being, that if you follow the *trend*, then it's worth noting that the lovely woman's name Merle means blackbird in poetic English, and if you wish, then in French as well, though the latter version does not seem to be as *in*.

HOPELESSLY NATURAL

Frostwork or "ice flowers" on a windowpane elude description. Look at the frosty patterns, dear readers, for they are sure to appear on your window at some time! Look at the window of a shed, veranda, or cottage that hasn't been heated for a while, on the panes of a bus shelter, or look at the ones pictured here. Look carefully and then try to image yourself describing them to an East Indian, an Aboriginal somewhere in Australia's heartland, or to the inhabitant of a leaf-hut in a rainforest, who has seen monkeys large and small, but never a windowpane that is alive.

Imagine that you're explaining to them – with the help of an interpreter, naturally – what frostwork is and how it silently and secretly appears, or doesn't appear, as the winter's cold sets in. And then also what the patterns look like on the glass and what they're made of and how. Such is the assignment. Almost as simple as writing something for a reader who has studied hundreds or thousands of various frost patterns since childhood on all manner of windows and has perhaps melted a peep-hole through them with their breath or warm fingertip in the tram or bus. It's amazing what's possible, thanks to the fact that someone invented panes of glass.

The kitchen door of our tiny home had a patterned square of glass that you could not see through. Under no circumstances was the kitchen door ever to be shut with a bang. That kind of frosted glass, if the boys had broken it, was not to be found during the war or afterwards. It was said to be the work of glass-smiths and very expensive. Maybe it was. In any case, when looked at closely, the kitchen door's glass was much more interesting and unique than the undulating, uneven glass surface of windowpanes, yet not nearly as beautiful as undulating glass covered with storybook frostwork, which was always born anew, was unique and fascinating and varied in a way no one can invent or predict. It was like a vision from the Creator, like Sass Suuman's "hopelessly natural nature", as he wrote in one of his poems many years later.

TRUST

In the middle of the harshest February, a redbreast appeared as if out of nowhere. The robin is a tiny bird, who is sometimes able to survive here until the end of October, but if you believe the bird guides, then it can occasionally spend the winter on Estonia's western islands as well. And this is exactly what happened a few years ago on the island of Hiiumaa, in Õngu: one morning a robin was crouched on a snowy step, staring up at people. It had most likely survived the heart of winter by an open stream somewhere nearby, finding a lone bug, or perhaps even catching a tiny fish, but now the situation had worsened. Feed me!

The bird's instincts were right. Operation "Chick" was immediately launched. But you cannot feed a redbreast sunflower seeds, breadcrumbs or crushed barley. Phones started ringing and agents were on the case. Whoever arrived from Tallinn was to bring along mealworms from the pet store, a hundred grams for a hundred kroons. The chick became a greater attraction than all the people visiting the nearby fish hatchery. No one knew where the robin spent the night, but come morning, it was whirling above the head of the first person to step outside – feed me!

It's curious to see a robin eating out of someone's hand. It's unusual to experience the close proximity of a tiny wild creature. For years, I've worked hard to live with the feeling of shame of belonging to my species. Humans are the only species of animal capable of wiping other species off the planet and the only one that has in fact done so. No matter where I show up, and no matter how good my intentions, it's always the same: someone escapes screeching, someone else hides away. I can crouch down to watch busy bees on blossoms, or ants bustling on the roadside, but it's better if it don't. Look at the eyes of a sparrow at a café, as it spies the piece of cake on your plate. No trust, absolutely none. And now this robin is sitting peacefully on a branch and looking at you straight on from a distance of half a metre. You direct the camera lens towards it, which a crow cannot tolerate from 100 metres, but the redbreast doesn't fly away. Doesn't fly away today, tomorrow or the next day. Doesn't even fly away after a week. You finally get used to it, but not completely. Someone trusts you. And something is not quite right. Something gets mixed up. Not in your head, no not there. In your soul.

THE MOON

The moon rises up in the sky and should this happen in the evening or by night, then one thing's for sure – if it's clear, there is no way it can keep its ascent a secret. Perhaps this is sometimes possible by day, when you suddenly notice – oh, the moon's out as well! If that's all the attention it merits by day, night is a different story. Moonlight is something more than simply the moon's light. Moonlight is the spell of light.

I can no longer recall how old I might have been, when I was awakened in the middle of the night by the howling of a dog. I stumbled out of bed and saw a huge beast of a dog, who knows where from, sitting in the middle of the road in front of our house and howling, snout full tilt towards the heavens, up at the moon. It was the saddest lament I've ever heard, and it distressed me to the point of angst and chills.

Why this dog, a stranger to our neighbourhood, and why our house and below my window? High in the night sky sat the mute, full moon and in its glow the street and potato field by the railway and train station and everything familiar on the other side of the tracks appeared totally different. The night seemed filled with mysterious omens, waiting their turn to be fulfilled. Perhaps a more recent fear of full moons has cast a shadow on this childhood memory. During the war, nights with a full moon meant possible bombing raids – on clear nights, the old lady who lived below did nothing but pray.

Later at school, I asked my science teacher why dogs howl at the moon. The teacher lapsed into a thorough lecture on the emotional and spiritual disposition of dogs. After all, what else can a dog do when it sees a large, bright, motionless spot in the night sky, which makes no noise and – what's most puzzling for dogs – has no odour! But not all dogs howl at the moon for the same reason that not all boys ask such questions. And so the dog-howling notion became a bit clearer. What also became clearer was why I myself might sometimes enjoy being a dog in the middle of a deserted road, to then point my snout at the sky and lighten my load by howling out my inner feelings towards something unknown and mysterious, since howling towards people is rarely of any help.

Luna, my companion of sleepless nights, oh how you change the world and wreak havoc with our senses! I've stared at your face in light and shadow, your ashy glow and crescent to the left and right, I've seen your comings and goings, listened to you in music and in the rhythmic murmurs of high tide on the ocean shore, but a mystery thou shall remain. Please do!

This close-up of the moon is but one of my many moon pictures. It and all the others were taken from the ground. Indeed, we can photograph the moon from closer still, but that is for other men with other instruments. My moon is the one that rises from beyond the treetops to pour bewitching light upon the world and have her way with our mortal souls.

THE LIGHT OF LOVE

I received a beautiful book of poetry for my birthday. The book is entitled "Armastuse valgus" – The Light of Love.

I picked up the gift one evening and began reading. The house was quiet and the street was quiet and as the night advanced, so the silence expanded. It was close to four o'clock, when I put the book down and turned off the light.

A gleam; a familiar, fine glow remains from that night, and I'm aware of signs of its trembling to this day.

It's like the smell of spring, which suddenly surprises you one morning or evening. An indistinguishable mix of melting snow, mounds of earth and expectant birches, so primal and mysterious that even the wind dare not dispel it.

This gleam, this smell, brings to mind a moment from my boyhood long ago. I was standing in the snow, my feet were wet and I was listening to the blackbird's song for the first time. I rested my back up against a birch tree and closed my eyes.

The bird kept on singing and I listened and thought that this was how one becomes blessed. Then the bird suddenly stopped and flew away with a loud screeching.

When I opened my eyes, I saw the sky above the trees. It wasn't quite an evening sky, it was rather that which precedes the evening, or is early evening, and its glow filled the western sky and the entire landscape. It was an aromatic glow.

There was something beyond what was perceivable through the senses; there was something that deeply touched that young boy's soul.

Occasionally that glow appears and it doesn't necessarily happen on a March evening, or at the edge of a wood with birds singing, but rather at a most unexpected moment and mysterious manner, as is appropriate for visions.

And in my thoughts I lean my boyhood back against the trunk of a birch and close my eyes, so when opening them again I can sense the amazing purity of that March long ago. For there is hardly a purer time in our year, than early March.

BACK AT MUSTJÕE

Wise books have written that animals come back to where they were born, or where their first offspring were born. Though not true of all animals, salmon, for instance, travel back to the rivers of their birth to spawn. And why could this not hold true for some human animals?

I stood on the banks of Mustjõe (the Black River) for the first time one evening long ago. So long ago, it feels like yesterday. I spent the night in a hayshed and made a small fire on a hillock beneath some trees. I could smell the molehills that had just melted out from beneath the snow at the bottom of the valley and the call of a lone night bird in the silence of the forest wall on the opposite bank seemed to come from another world. Smoke from the fire crawled along the river valley and disappeared behind the bend. What a bewitching moment. I was taken aback. I would never have thought that Estonia was so beautiful.

I left my soul there that night. Something happened. Perhaps it was the birth of a boy in his sixteenth year. Travels to many other corners of Estonia have been nothing more than journeys to this bend in the river to revisit my soul. I know that it's in a safe place. Life has no doubt tried to grapple it, but has never reached it to bruise it.

It would be disastrous to lose the path to your soul. You must take care, so the path does not become overgrown, or buried in trash.

MARCH ICE

The Inuit and Yupik, or Eskimo of the Russian Far East, are thought to greet each other by rubbing noses when they meet. I wonder if this is in fact true, and if they do rub, do they rub up and down, or right to left? I haven't remembered to investigate this further, but I do recall that when I showed a female schoolmate how the Eskimoan people reportedly greet, I witnessed something completely extraordinary. Having quietly watched the girl every day, I knew the lines of her face down to the last detail, dark eyes and arched brows, but I had never before seen her so close-up. What I now saw was the real her and someone else as well – beautiful, unknown, new, endlessly mysterious. I was shocked, not so much by the never-before-seen newness of the familiar face, but by the exhilaratingly unusual experience. Later on, I continued to try to observe people's faces close up in this way, sometimes as if almost by accident, sometimes on purpose and even brazenly.

I wouldn't say the world always looks wonderful up-close, but it is surely interesting and different, whether it be a human face or chunk of stone; the wing of a dragonfly, a toadstool or leaf. The Creator's creation is unfathomable. It sometimes makes no difference whether you're witnessing a landscape seen from kilometres on high, or patches of micro-lichens on tree bark. Beautiful rosettes and intriguing maps of unknown countries can be found atop fieldstones and the work of the ice-flower gardener on a windowpane is endlessly fascinating. The world in a drop of water. Blades of grass in a row. Ripples on a sandy beach.

I have hundreds of photos of ice. Sharp cold needles on stalks in burnt-out fields and melt-in-your-mouth icicles, gossamer lace by barely seeping water and piles by the seashore as high as a house. One divider sheet in my ice photos binder reads MARCH ICE. March ice is a special kind of ice, in the way that a distinct western wind blows only from the west and thundershowers only fall to the ground from clouds. There are different types of March ice, from completely clear to porous, full of an inner sparkle and shimmer. Yet in one respect, March ice is always the same: if you press your nose up against it and look closely, you can see the coming of spring.

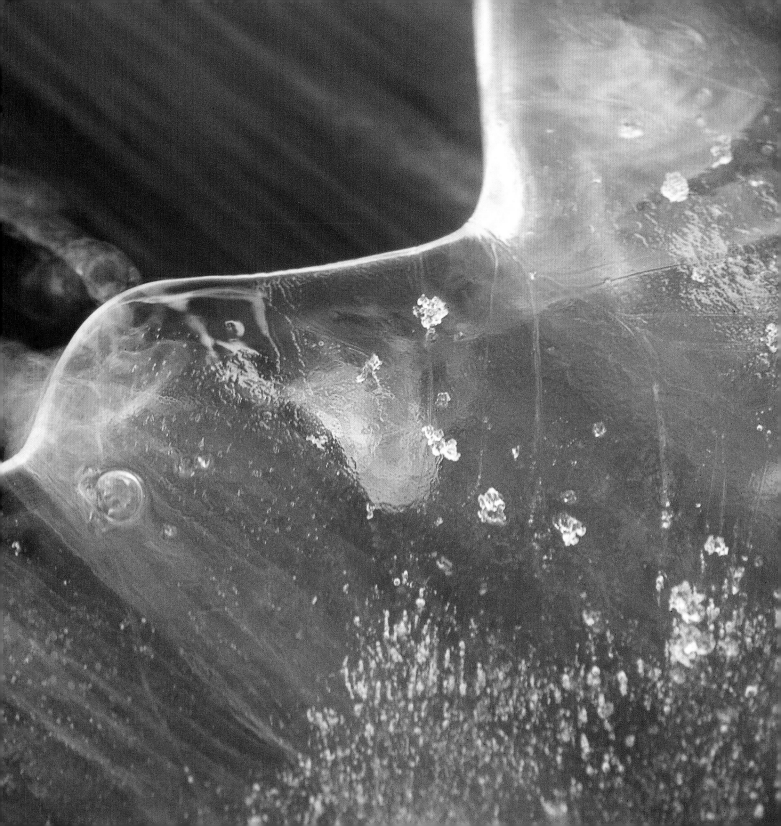

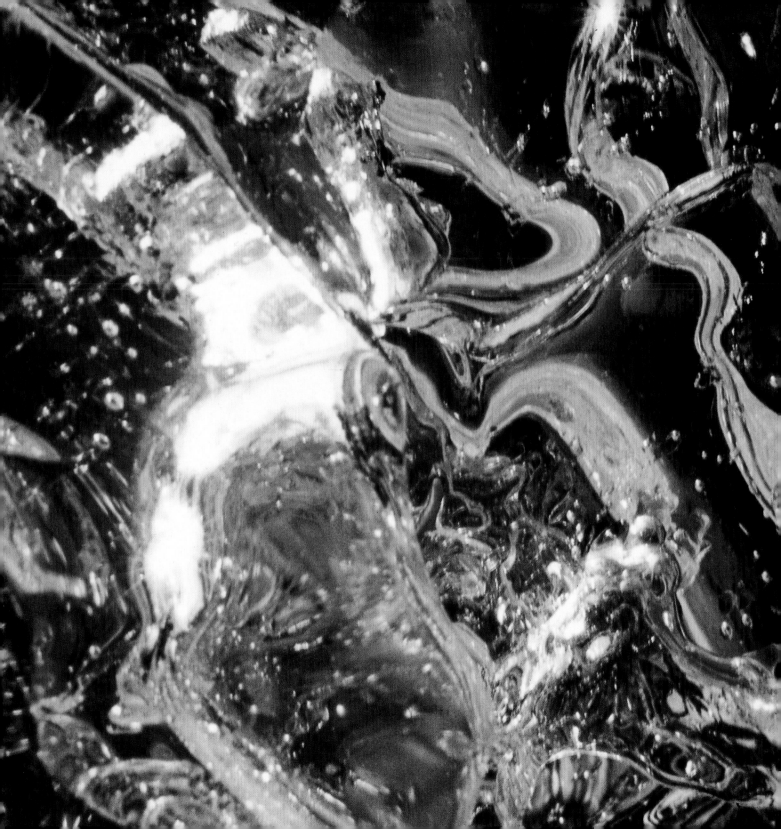

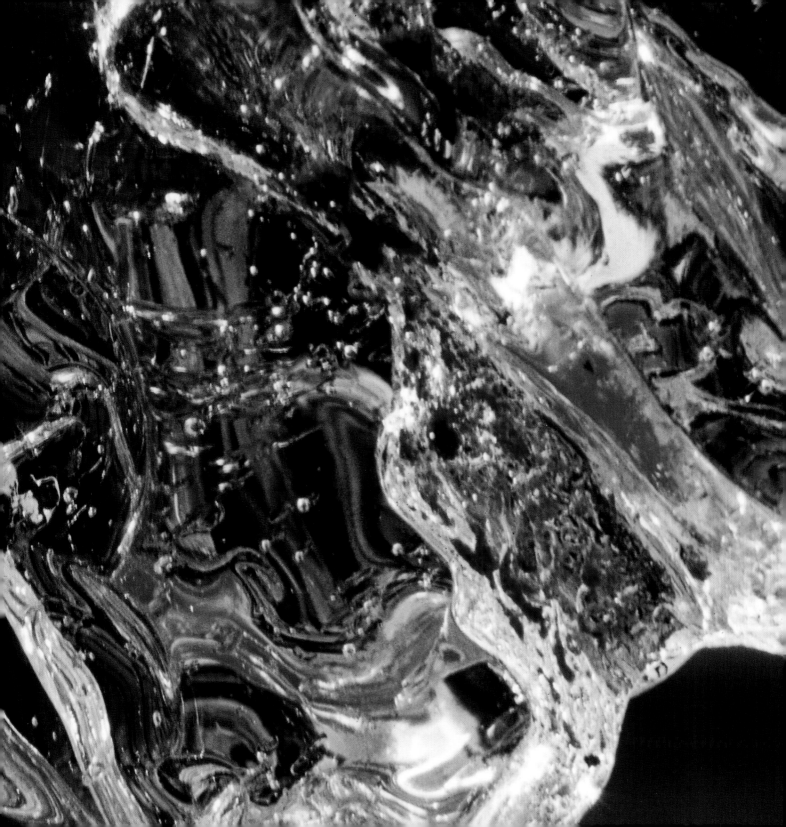

THE GREAT WATER

It was known that the day would come when the rivers stand over their banks once again. And it was presumed this would occur in April. But now it seems as if there is an endless amount of water – icy, brown water in slow, dignified motion that is hard to put into words.

Jänijõgi (the Jäni River) in the forests of the Kõrvemaa region is but a small river, yet in early spring it becomes very large. Just as it's impossible to measure joy or sadness with a hourglass, the river is not a absolute barometer of events.

Yet the great water is in itself an event. A brief moment in spring, when the water of a small river becomes great. It fills up the flat river valley and floods the forest floor on both sides of the riverbed. I haven't seen chunks of ice jostling noisily downriver here. There are larger and smaller pieces, which are unwillingly pulled along by the current and are happiest settling on a hillock or side of a bank to melt.

These waters are not able to budge the larger sheets of ice. Trickles and twisters develop between the pieces and the entire river valley is filled with a merry gurgling. This creates a beautiful backdrop for the songs of the robin and song thrush. Towards evening, when the birds grow quiet, there is only the gurgling; a river valley full of happy babbling. Amazing!

I chanced onto the banks of the flooded Jänijõgi for the first time half a century ago. At the time, the Kõrvemaa river valleys opened up to reveal some of the most beautiful cultivated landscapes I had ever seen in Estonia. These were meadows, which were carefully cleared of brush and mowed yearly. Like a natural park. The hay was placed in sheds and was carried out when the sledge paths were driven in. There were sheds at every bend in the river and there was always enough hay in some of them to spend the night whenever necessary.

I built my fire pit near one of the sheds, beneath some tall pines. There I would sit by the fire. I would catch crayfish in August, listen to the night sounds in early spring and watch the floodwater on the bottom of the river valley. I didn't think about the fact that the water seeped from the forests and bogs and finally flowed into the sea – I sensed it. That brownish water that came from somewhere and went somewhere else: in an unhurried and dignified manner, without the slightest hesitation, as if following the highest order. If you keep watching this endless movement intently and long enough, it will carry you along with it. And then it's as if you too have been given the highest, eternal laws to abide by.

Sometimes the river rises over its banks during the fall rains as well, but that's different than in spring. That is not the Great Water – it doesn't announce the coming of light.

SPARROW

A sparrow, eye cocked strangely fro, walks amongst the honest folk... And the honest folk and blackbirds, gardeners and other figures, us and you as well, look poorly upon the sparrows, as if saying: "Look, the grabbers are here too, vying for the honestly obtained property of others."

Actually there are two such cockeyed greedy boys, the house sparrow and the tree sparrow. Both are a kind of human creation, whereas the house sparrow is thought to have come to us from the Middle East and the tree sparrow from China.

The sparrow does indeed go hand in hand with humans. Humans set its table and without them nothing would have come of the sparrows conquering the world. Goethe has said that it is only possible to live side by side with one's own kind and not even, because who is able to stand their own kind? This is more or less how the neighbourly relations of these so-called grey coats, or shedkeepers, or plowmen have played out. As far as the sparrow is concerned, people could live in peace, but people don't care for the eating habits of their neighbours. In China, they decided to set the house rules straight in the middle of the last century. Three million Chinese battled the sparrows for three days. Millions of birds were killed, but instead of the expected increase in rice crops, there was a decrease, since the insect pests took more than the sparrows ever did. There was no other choice than to bring on the guests and the guests's bread!

And so this is how we share our living space, with the sparrow grabbing bites from our table, while we watch in awe at the decisiveness and audacity with which this takes place. But I have yet to meet a sparrow who will eat out of your hand. Humans cannot be trusted, truly cannot, and the sparrow knows this.

It's April and the sparrow bushes are abuzz. There is a general flurry of activity in the meadows and between houses. Mates are wooed and fights are fought over females and real estate. Great things are happening and they need to be arranged. Steel and glass does not suit the sparrow, they like houses in old neighbourhoods with holes in the outer boards and all kinds of nooks and spaces. Some pairs settle as subletters in the hollows of a stork's nest, a nice safe place. They must be able to raise two broods, because time flies and life is short – a year or two at best. An average of six tree sparrows out of a thousand live to the age of five and only one reaches the age of six. Naturally there are exceptions: supposedly the oldest house and tree sparrows have lived to the age of thirteen. Humans, with their unpredictable ways of life and poisons, cats and predatory birds, as well as mysterious diseases set the rules here. Thankfully there is an expression that promises: weeds don't disappear.

SOMETHING ALIVE

Something beautiful, soul quenching and sincere, sometimes even something funny can appear when nature has defrosted and the waters begin rushing. The tit's song and crow's call can then be heard everywhere, but this certain something beautiful should be a thing that doesn't come straight to you and is not quite everyday. It should be something that you search for, in order to then listen and watch. And at the same time, it would also be good if this something didn't take off shrieking, or escape like a shot when you've finally found it and settle down to study it.

There used to be a gigantic bomb crater near our vegetable patch in Tondi, between the old railway and Pärnu Highway – now it has long been covered in asphalt and concrete with monstrous buildings on top – but then it was in a damp meadow and stood brimming with water in the spring. So when the workers from the matchstick factory, mostly women, including our mother, gathered there to start with the first spring work, I snuck to the water's edge, placed a slab of tar paper under my stomach and lay down on the muddy edge to watch the frogs. At first the frogs escaped underwater, but soon rose to the surface one at a time and continued to go about their frog business – continued to spawn. Common frogs, known as grass frogs in Estonian, are not particularly shy. In fact they don't fear those interested in the least, if you sit patiently in one spot and don't make any sudden movements. You can spend hours like this and observe their activities from a distance of twenty centimetres or so, the main thing being that you rest on something dry. It's quite interesting to listen to the contemplative frog song. From a slight distance it is reminiscent of a purring cat settled in your lap, but close up it sounds like the droning of a motor. A quiet, but powerful sound, a manly single-toned drone, meaning only one thing and so irresistible… In those distant springs, after having stared at the frogs for many hours, it seemed as if they showed some interest in me as well: by their manner of coming and looking straight at you with their buggy eyes, quieting down, forgetting their panic, perhaps even having an opinion about you and you seem interesting to them since they, relaxed smiles and all, seem interesting to you. Forgive me, dear amphibians, but at the time, I really didn't know to think that your species is so easily wounded; so helpless and unprotected before that being, resting on the edge of the bomb crater with one ear in the frog world, justifying your existence to himself in his child mind and later, when trying to explain it to others, having to be so disappointed.

THE LAND OF SAARNAKI

One summer day long ago, when I stepped onto Saarnaki land for the first time, I thought that if paradise can be somewhere on earth then it's here. I had seen some islands before, but had to admire them from afar, always secretively. Islands were out of reach for us, they could only be approached by sombre, grey Soviet military boats. Even thinking about islands was a crime against the state. The only island I had previously visited – you could reach the island of Tauksi by foot through the sea – required me having to sign-in, like a farmer in 1955 referred to it, in a special notebook according to the strict orders of those in power. The families on Saarnaki had no such record book. Records of those visiting or studying the islands of the Väinameri, meaning "Sea of the Strait", between the mainland and west coast islands, were kept elsewhere. One could only be in this area since the Väinameri was a *tōl* or rear in Soviet border guard jargon.

Yes, islands are wonderfully mystical. There are a total of 1500 islands in our waters and not all of them are mystical, but some are.

The small island of Saarnaki is particularly mystical. I'm referring to that feeling of paradise, which many people experience when they arrive on an island for the first time, but which no one is really able to explain. It's like a spell. Living and working on the island of Hiiumaa and visiting it later, I believed I was getting used to the magical powers of Saarnaki, but I was kidding myself. Now, when I end up there alone, I'm once again under its spell. Sometimes this spell appears as the spring trill of a whimbrel, sometimes the clatter of a long-forgotten, non-existent mower can be heard through the roar of the sea, or the sounds of people and snorting of horses. The twittering of hundreds of swallows, playing of instruments and buzz of June beetles fill the summer air. The smell of bread fresh out of the oven...

But when May arrives, the land of Saarnaki glows yellow with cowslips. Even today. Really-truly, even now!

Blessed be springtime in Estonia!

THE HOOTER

People talk about the wailing of night birds. Some may whoop or wail, but the ural owl, like the one on this photo, definitely hoots rather that whoops. Its hooting can be hear in the dark forest in the evening, at night and in the early morning and it's as if someone was asking an important question: *Yoohoo, are the girls home?* That is at least how local people have heard the ural owl calling in the past. The ural owl is not seen very often, but in years with fewer mice, an empty stomach makes the owl active by day as well, and then it occasionally chances by a highway to be seen by passers-by.

However, this owl is heard and seen quite often in the forests of Estonia (less frequently on the islands, true enough), since it's not a very rare bird in our area. And the ural owl is also curious: it comes by the campfire at night and stares at those sitting around the fire from its high perch. It has even happened, that while flying by a house, an owl has tried to peer inside through a window or open door, as if to say, what are they doing there, by the lamplight?! If a ural owl begins nesting in the hollow of a tree in the yard or somewhere close to the house, then you must give it its peace. You must in fact take great care, especially in May when the chicks have grown, because if its threatening beak-clacking is not heeded, the bird can attack with lightening speed and an owl's flight is noiseless and its talons needle-sharp. I know two one-eyed ornithologists...

But more about the one here on the pine bough. One June night years ago, he came to my campsite by the Loobu River. For fun, I asked if the girls were home. He took offence. Flew away, but was soon back with his woman. Fussed around the tent until morning and then I took this picture of his majesty. I listened to the owl couple's screeches and hollow hootings and pondered that they were like messages from another world. A world I believed I truly belonged to as a boy and where I felt completely happy. Until a Woman – here with a capital letter – snapped me out of it, just like mother had once predicted, using a cautionary tone. I wonder how long this time of joy would've lasted, or what would've followed, if I had not been moved by a woman's enchantment?

THE SMELL OF GREEN

People are thought to have sensed the mystical nature of ferns as far back as the dawn of their being. My first experience with ferns was full of mystery and its memory stretches back to the beginnings of my life as I know it. It's not by chance that people say the life path of humans is in many ways similar to their evolutionary path.

It was like this. The three of us, my mother, brother and myself, travelled to Tapa for a visit. My mother's brother, uncle Ets, lived in Tapa with his family. I must have been four at the time, because uncle Ets was still alive then, but he was killed in a bombing raid soon after the war began. At Tapa, we first ate and drank and then took some baskets and went out strawberry picking. Uncle Ets made small cups out of birch bark for the children to pick their berries into.

We spent a long day in the forest. The adults were busy picking and we drank jam-water out of bottles. Then it began to thunder and we sought shelter from the rain at a nearby farm. It was really hot in their kitchen and there were a lot of flies and the shepherd boy showed off his noisy wooden rattle. I have not seen or heard such a rattle for scaring the herd since. But does this have anything to do with ferns? Sure it does!

The baskets stood by the wall on the floor. When the rain stopped and our group prepared to set out, I saw that the baskets were full of berries to the brim, but were covered with fern leaves, so you almost couldn't see the strawberries. I knelt down by the biggest basket to study it a bit further and was struck by a unique, strong odour. The basket smelled red and green. I already knew the red smell – strawberries, and my fingers smelled red, but the green smell was new and stuck in my mind. I later told my mother about the green smell that rose from the basket along with the red, but I shouldn't have. She said it was silly talk, because a smell cannot possibly be green and I couldn't understand why my mother didn't understand, that this smell could not possibly be green, it simply IS green. If not even my mother could understand that the world around us, when arranged with the help of learned knowledge, does have a deeper and indescribable meaning, then there is no point waiting for understanding from anyone or anywhere else.

From that time on, whenever I find myself in a fern wood on a warm day, I take in deep breaths of the green smell. There are hundreds of other scents, but what of them! There's no point, because all those smells are tied to the green smell and this is all silly talk anyway.

All the same, times have changed and people hopefully have as well and that is why I must mention one final and very crucial detail: the strawberry baskets in that farm kitchen near Tapa were covered with lady ferns. Fairytales of magical blossoming ferns pale in comparison.

THE WAIT

If you wish to see something new, choose a familiar path.

Today the path led me to the sand on the seashore. The sea has been far offshore for weeks and all kinds of folks are on the move on the expanse of sand left behind. A fox went to the water's edge collecting dead fish. Two swans have waddled straight across the open plain. Seagulls and oystercatchers have been searching for life in the puddles.

And suddenly this unexpected piece of news: a pair of little terns are flying nervously above my head, calling out. I've never seen these birds here before. I study the area carefully and soon find the reason for their anxiety: three eggs on the barren sand. Here lie the entire earthly possessions of these graceful starling-sized coastal birds. This is their everything. The time of falling in love and playing games is past, now is the time for care and anticipation.

As a young boy I loved to look for birds' nests. I still enjoy searching for them. When it's possible, I peer into the nest, to see what's inside. The young often tend to look similar, so nests with eggs are more interesting: to see what colour and shape, how many and whether large or small.

I look at the eggs on the sand and a discussion in a children's story comes to mind. What does a bird's egg tell us? What is its true secret? What would we find out about the egg, if we took it out of the nest and broke it? We would discover that the delicate shell is protecting the egg yolk and white. And that's it.

But let's leave the nest alone and take some time to wait. If you're very patient, then we can see how a miracle unfolds: soon a weak, helpless and naked baby bird breaks out of the shell. Let's wait a bit more. Then we shall see how the baby birds begin to carry their heads, grow, develop and liven up; we see how they outgrow the nest and prepare to stretch their wings, until finally they fly out of the nest into the great wide world.

Sometimes during beautiful September mornings, I go wandering along forest paths to listen to the first vocal attempts of young warblers or wren boys. Wow, is it ever hard to keep a tune, when you have yet to master the note. They are like young cocks struggling to crow.

Then the birds grow quiet and fall comes, then winter, the anticipation of spring and finally spring once more.

And perhaps one day a young tern will once again spread its graceful wings, thereby revealing the secret of today's egg to me. I await the wonder of this secret, this nature.

Time and patience, my dears. All too often it happens that we break something delicate and beautiful because we cannot bear to wait for time to reveal its secret to us with care and love.

WOODED MEADOW

I suppose I had seen some wooded hayfields before, but the first time I saw a true western Estonian wooded meadow was in the summer of 1955 at the age of twenty. I took a break from my tedious fieldwork at Puiste and went off wandering. By nightfall I reached some acquaintances near Ridala. Scythes were being sharpened on a grindstone in the yard and one was placed aside for me as well. I sensed that I didn't know how to mow. I was told: "You will by tomorrow night."

And so it was. I struggled for half a day and struck the blade in the turf, but in the afternoon I was given a new scythe and swath, or mowing path, beside the others. And I sharpened the scythe on a whetstone myself. And so on until dusk. Before heading home, we gathered around the cut flax to stretch out a bit and slurp the buttermilk left over from lunch. The meadow where we swung our scythes all day has stuck in my memory as one of the most glorious landscapes I have ever seen. I shall never forget the smells of that night long ago. The smell of birches and oaks, the smell of mowed and un-mowed hay and the smell of something else, but I'm not sure what. The air made your senses giddy. If someone had told me that night, that there will come a time, when such land will be brought back to life with the help of foreign funds, then I wouldn't have known what to think.

Wooded meadows are beautiful. I've mowed hay there. I've taken photos there. And I've daydreamed there. I've admired them all around the Baltic Sea, but I'm most in awe of the extraordinary richness of Estonian wooded meadows: 76 different types of plants were found one summer on one square metre of land on the Laelatu wooded meadow near Virtsu!

I like the idea that if we had to choose a national landscape, that it could well be the wooded meadow. Our people have always been linked to this landscape. Hay and leaved switches for animals, axe handles, rake teeth, and all manner of wood for household items came from here – the warmth of the house. People went to such a meadow to work, pick flowers and listen to birds singing. The lines of a popular song say, "This is just the wooded meadow for having a party…".

Dear new era, please make it so, that wooded meadows don't disappear from Estonia forever.

THE SEA SWALLOW

If Swan Lake had been frozen, Tchaikovsky would not have written his infamous ballet. Maia Plissetskaja had to take time and care to observe the swan swimming in the lake or pond, before she began dancing the part of the dying swan. Similarly, I am not able to imagine a swan waddling on the grass or amongst tussocks when listening to Saint-Saëns's "The Swan". The secret to the Japanese's very unique bowing, which is always accompanied by smiles, was revealed to me when I saw a video of a Japanese crane's dance at the Kushiro City Museum. I had previously seen these birds dancing on the movie screen, but I hadn't realised at the time, that humans could also bow as beautifully as the cranes. People watch the movement or movements of animals and say "magnificent", "graceful", or "stylish". They would also like to fly like an eagle or swallow and step as gracefully as a deer, but not stomp on the dance floor like a bear, or stumble like a wooden horse. Indeed, nature offers both enticing and cautionary examples, without being majestic or graceful or stylish or trendy, but remaining as nature, its true self, and not allowing itself to be influenced in the slightest by anyone's vision or interpretation.

It's summer. Let us stop on the beach to watch the tern's limber flight. Coastal inhabitants have many names for the noisy and quarrelsome tern, including "sea swallow," since its long wings and majestic forked-tail are similar to that of a swallow. The tern's nest is somewhere amongst the rocks or in the grass, but we won't go looking for it, because the bird may give us a peck on the head. But the tern's flight is always a joy to observe. We have no other such flyer, nor does the rest of the world. The Arctic tern arrives here from its wintering grounds in Antarctica. From there it flies to nest on some of the most northerly patches of ice-free land. The length of the Arctic tern's journey from the seas of the Antarctic to the Arctic is 16 000 kilometres. An Arctic tern chick, unable to fly at the time, was banded on the coast of Labrador and was found 90 days later 14 400 kilometres away on the south-east coast of Africa; another flew to south-eastern Africa from Greenland, 16 000 kilometres away. All imaginable flight records of the bird kingdom were broken by an Arctic tern's flight from the Arctic to Australia – 22 000 kilometres!

But what do we know of records in the bird kingdom and what do terns care, they just keep flying.

THE FIRST BUTTERFLY

In some years, the wonder of the butterfly reveals itself as early as March. This wonder is in the butterfly itself – the colourful tortoiseshell sunning itself in the corner of the garden, or the sulphur yellow brimstone butterfly by the wood's edge. On occasion, the wind carries them into the frenzied city, heralding the approach of summer to the city folk as well. Should a motley butterfly be the first to arrive, the summer proposes to be colourful and rich in adventure, but if it's yellow, the summer will be golden. As spring flourishes and summer blooms, the butterfly community becomes more colourful still.

Yes, butterflies are beautiful. They are beautiful even if not so very colourful or mottled. Butterflies grab your attention and capture your awe and passion. They are bought and sold, gifted and exchanged. Dead. Butterflies are big business and a thorn in the side of collectors whose passions need quelling. Butterfly houses have been opened in many parts of the world; they are like butterfly zoos of sorts. Just buy your ticket and enter the glass bubble of a tropical world where bright, exotic species fly about you, some so large, you can hear the flapping of their wings. Production occurs on the spot. You can observe from beyond the glass how these wonders emerge from their cocoons and become butterflies. Literature about them is all you get to take home with you.

Nine hundred varieties of larger butterflies and more than a thousand small species have been identified in Estonia. During the day, we primarily see day butterflies, who love the sun and hide away on grey and rainy days. At dusk the night butterflies emerge. Summer is the time for butterflies.

What remains of a butterfly on the windshield of a moving car is but a nasty splatter. It's not known how many butterflies die on our highways. Hoards die in puddles of rainwater where they stop to drink. They are enticed to sit on roads for unknown reasons. And that is where many will remain.

Cycling through Hiiumaa one summer day, I spotted three purple emperor butterflies in the roadside dust. I didn't see a single one alive and flying about, rare as they tend to be in these parts. I picked them up, as I always do if they're still whole. I later study them more carefully under my magnifying glass, to see the unexpected and photograph them close-up. Sometimes their wing patterns are like stained glass windows, sometimes like the wonderland viewed from an airplane.

Even kaleidoscope memories from childhood cannot match this hidden beauty. Who can you ask why they are pieced together just so and not some other way? Nature is not accountable to man and asks not what man thinks or feels; nature has its own internal laws.

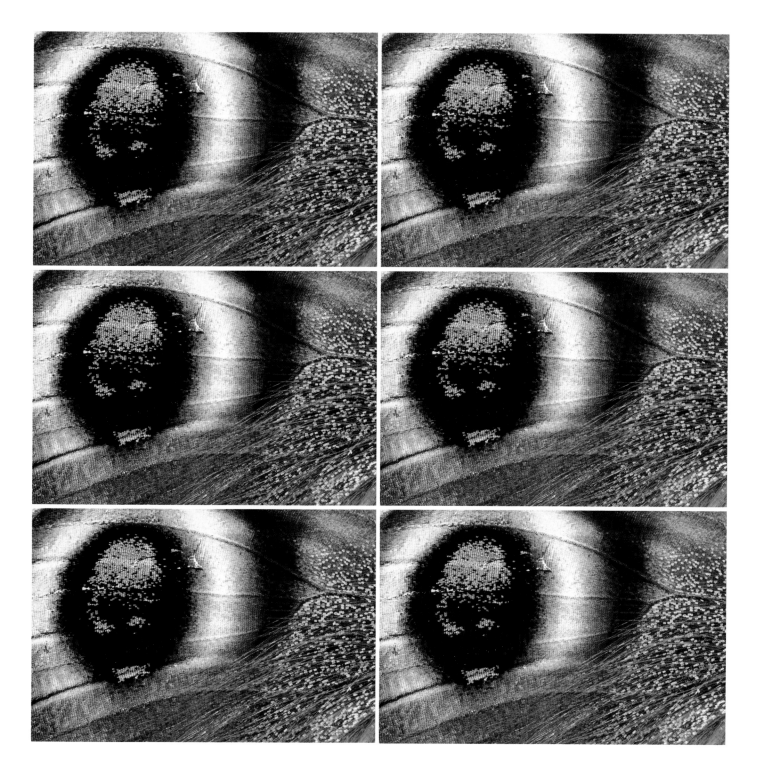

OLD TREES

It was mid-summer. The oaks of Kadrioru Park rose to the sky. I held my mother's hand and stared at the emerald green crowns of trees towering above my head, casting quivering shadows on the road in the light of midday. Is it possible, that there are really trees this big?

We had begun our walk by the Swan Pond, where the fountain sent shimmering jets of water sky-high, but what is a pond, when compared to such green trees! I had seen nothing even remotely close to this on the island of my birth, oceans away.

This may have been one of our first walks to Kadriorg. Mother had found temporary lodging with an old woman on the barren limestone ridge of Lasnamäe and it was a quick jaunt down the hill of the Song Festival Grounds to go explore in the park.

We often visited Kadriorg later as well. When we moved down from Lasnamäe, we would travel there by tram. In the fall, the parks trees turned yellow and red. During the time of falling leaves it was fun to rustle your feet in the leaf-carpet.

The years grew on, but Kadriorg's old trees remained. They were the centre of much activity, which we studied as schoolboys and made presentations about in nature clubs – these birds and those bugs, on the trees, under the trees and in the trees.

I've now been living for decades in the Kadrioru area. A ten minute walk and you're in the park. When our children were small, they too rustled their feet in the fall leaves and were in awe of the squirrel's games and the tits who came to grab a snack from the palm of your hand. And one thing was for sure: when in Kadriorg, we always went to wander and take pictures under the big trees.

While there, we were usually quiet, everyone with their own thoughts.

Old trees are like old people. They exude peace and dignity. They create peace and order in the whole. That's why I go to listen to the quiet, eloquent musings of old linden and oaks even now. Why do some people not like old trees, I wonder? Is it really because they outlive us?

you can redo all my pictures
you yourselves know well which ones
but I wouldn't want for you to fell
the giant trees behind the house

Jüri Üdi "A Letter to Brothers"

THE ICEBREAKER

The icebreaker is that long-footed "thick-legged Thomas", with legs that are in fact hair-thin, who is out breaking, knocking and stomping the sun-warmed April ice on the river and the sea, bobbing its long tail up and down all the while. The Finns say that a wagtail breaks more ice with its thin legs than a thousand sturgeon fishermen. There are reports that it is in fact this flax bird who pushes the Pärnu River ice off with its knee.

If this bird was first seen flying high or sitting on a rooftop in the spring, then you could expect a good year for flax, but seeing it on the ground or low down, predicted a poor and weak crop. This is the wagtail's link to flax and this knowledge was shared by other peoples related to us. In the fall, we see the white wagtail catching the last flies by a sunny warm wall as late as October. In the meanwhile, it has succeeded in raising two broods of chicks and perhaps even a cuckoo.

The white wagtail is one of the first birds that I remember seeing scurrying on the manure pile behind the barn on my aunt's small farm while the swallows chattered on the clothesline in the yard. We can find the white wagtail in all landscapes, only dense forests are not to their liking. And no other bird has more nicknames than this wagtail – no less than sixty!

This wagtail is small, but tough enough to attack larger birds when they wander into its territory. Sometimes it will even chase a hawk. But if a white wagtail steps up to fight itself in front of a window or side mirror of a car, then it's wise to cover the mirror up, because this battle will not wane. Which by no means suggests that the wagtail is not suitable for co-operative work with other birds. It is one of our most frequent adoptive cuckoo parents and if you believe the bird guides, then the wagtail has also helped raise the young of other songbirds and wagtails chicks have in turn been fed by sparrows.

A pair of wagtails nesting in the crevice of a wall, woodpile or stone fence gets along quite well with humans, but not at all with cats. White wagtails get along famously with us, my dear readers, since we are kind and attentive towards birds and allow them to live in peace.

THE SKY

I'm lying on the heath, surrounded by blossoming heather and the buzzing of bees.

I'm staring at the sky. I stare at the sky in summer and winter, in spring and fall, but I most enjoy watching the movements of clouds in the August sky. You look: at first there's nothing, then suddenly a small shred of cloud appears above the heath. It starts gaining strength and growing, so that soon its shadow blankets all the surrounding hillocks. Now you wait for the cloud to immediately spread itself across the entire sky, but it doesn't, instead it starts changing shape by seemingly spinning around itself and shredding at the edges and now it looks like a completely different cloud. But in a moment – what a miracle! – the cloud disappears altogether.

It's a joy to watch the movement of the powers of the sky. Sometimes swallows fly around busily beneath the clouds, but the clouds themselves are unpredictable, especially when you observe them with children. Then the expanse is full of the movements of lions and sheep and angels, or they all pile up into mountains no one has ever seen before and will never see again.

The sky cannot be rushed or held back, told what to do, directed or scolded, since things in the sky work according to the rules of the sky. Swallows come and go, the sky was and is.

Sometimes the sky makes you restless, it can even make you downright anxious. That's when you look at the face of your loved one and suddenly see lions and sheep and angels, you see someone stretching their tremendous paw across the expanse, see distant perplexing mountains and you have no idea what secrets may be locked within. That is when you look into the face of your loved one, but have forgotten that you are watching the sky, which you cannot restrain or give orders to, speed up or hold back, buy or sell; you've forgotten, that even here things go their own way, according to the laws of the skies, over which you cannot have any say or power now or ever.

You must take the time to look up at the sky. The sky has might and power, otherwise Estonians of old would not have believed that: "The sky wanted it so."

A MIRACLE OF NATURE

Of course it's a miracle, this cross spider's web, because it simply IS miraculous. A spider's web is particularly magical at dawn on a dewy August morning. Then it seems as if the myriad of pearl strings hanging from the bushes and grass have been placed there for the adornment of the fatherland and amazement of the people. They then fail to recall spiders hidden away in crevices and the creation of Nature and management of its affairs. Nor do people think about their place or responsibility within this order, but simply admire. This is how yet another miracle takes place. For how could miracles occur, if there was no one to marvel? Minerals are simply stones in the ground; some of them become precious stones thanks to jewellers, jewellery designers and others who treasure them. The people of Hiiumaa say: "God leads, a person searches."

But the story of the spider in its hiding place, or in the dewdrops on a web, is that she, Arachne (spider in Greek), was once a young girl, who achieved such prowess at weaving, that she invited the Goddess Athena herself to compete. As is always the case, this arrogance got its due punishment. Gods are not competed with. Athena did not recognise Arachne's worth and the despondent girl wanted to hang herself, but the Goddess turned her into a spider, who forever spins its web. And the spider weaves; it has woven for millions of years.

The spider's entire life has to do with threads. She prepares it out of silk produced in her own personal web factory, which knows no rivals. There are over twenty thousand species of these web weavers on all the continents, all masters in their own right and slaves to their instincts. If you were to imagine a spider's thread of silk as being 1 mm in diameter, then such a web could carry up to 260 kg of weight, but luckily Athena did not entrust such materials to Arachne. For what would the traps and cocoons be like then, or how would the wind be able to carry the sparkling frosty threads during Indian Summer, on which young spiders sail off into the world in search of their fortune.

Spider webs pearled with dew can be admired during calm weather. Such miracles cannot be born in storms; storms ravage those which already exist. Without peace, there is no point in counting on miracles. Not at home, in the meadow or anywhere on earth.

SWALLOW

I didn't want to catch a swallow... Of course you didn't, but see how everything can sometimes go the other way? Looking at how the national bird spreads its beautiful wings on the Estonian 500-kroon note, yet another line of poetry comes to mind: *Don't believe what the wolf says...* Oh, those poets – how is it that they're able to put everything so perfectly in style, as is customary for the people of the island of Hiiumaa to say.

Yes, we have these birds – swallows. Although they spend seven months far away, they're with us at home for five. It's arranged so that they build their nests and raise their young here. The Estonian word for swallow – pääsuke, is most likely an onomatopoetic word, which presents itself in many forms. The barn swallow or "smoke swallow" in Estonian, is the farm family's lucky bird and has gotten its name through German from smoky kitchens, where it would build its nest. But the house martin also lives in Estonia – it is a swallow of the beach, who moulds its clay home under a house's eaves or on coastal cliffs. Sand martins live in colonies in the steep, sandy embankments of rivers, lakes or sand and gravel pits. Neither house, nor sand martins have the forked tail or bubbly song of the swallow, nor do they have the red throat patch – the blood pudding thrown there by the lady of the house. Other swallows are also not as talented fliers. However, they are all loved and admired.

Swallows provide a lot of joy. I remember how, at the age of twelve, I collected tiny feathers in a Järvamaa farm chicken coop, enough to fill my palms and then spent hours sitting by the pond, blowing them in the air and watched how the swallows caught them in mid-flight and carried them to their nests in the barn or stall. There were also house martins and swifts (who aren't really swallows), but the most interesting was always the flight, song and carryings on of the barn swallows.

The swallow's nest of clay and grass stalks is the predecessor of iron-concrete and a very important part of its life is associated with its nest, starting in May until August, when they begin preparing to fly off. The later chicks are destined to perish, since their instinct to migrate is not able to develop sufficiently. The life of journeying swallows is harsh.

Just as the image of the swallow on the 500-kroon note has become notably diluted and paler over time, so too has the life of swallows.

The swallows' pre-journey gatherings are a great and important event, full of excitement. This is when the young swallows get their first lessons necessary for the flight to the tropics, or as far as southern Africa. These lessons need not necessarily take place on a weather vane showing the points of the compass, but it's certainly more impressive this way; at least to watch on a glorious August day.

KAIBALDI HEATH

The forest path becomes so sandy, that it's impossible to continue riding my bike. And further ahead there is only sand. I lean the bike up against a tree and continue on foot. Pines, increasingly feeble as I go along, and heather, nothing more. I take off my shoes and press my toes into the warm sand. Nice.

Barren land and silence. Pieces of unusually shaped, weather-bleached wood and dried pinecones are scattered about, in some spots the roots of the pines have been exposed. At the bottom of their sneaky funnels, ant lions await their pray unseen, a white wagtail has descended for a brief moment, taken a few dance steps here and there and flown away again. The beetle went about its beetle business and the fox did its thing. All of this is written on the sand of Kaibaldi heath. As well as the fact, that someone has driven around here. Always, when I come here, someone has inevitably driven on the sand with a car.

I discovered this spot with its unique atmosphere in the middle of Hiiumaa's heath forests decades ago. At that time, you could still find tree stumps resembling skeletons and hear the cooing of grouse in the spring. There used to be a Soviet army tank base at Kaibaldi. When the tanks were taken away from Hiiumaa, the churned-up land was left abandoned. Foresters no doubt made an attempt to plant pines here, but this first-aid hasn't really helped. Time heals all wounds and time passes slowly on infertile land.

I've sometimes wondered what might draw me here, but haven't yet been enlightened. I sit on the sun-warmed sand and look around – there really isn't anything to look at here. You listen – silence. Occasionally yes, a raven caws somewhere, then it's quiet once more. There are some days in life, when nothing really happens. Then it's like Kaibaldi heath. Simply beautiful. Most likely because it's so pure and clean. But it's especially beautiful on the sand here in August, because that's when the heather is abloom.

BALANCE

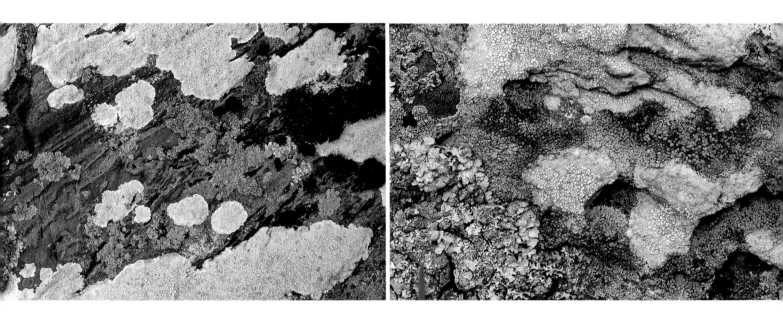

There's a rock on Haldi beach on the isle of Hiiumaa, that I have succeeded in remembering among all the countless rocks on the beach, so that if someone were to ask if I knew of a totally unique rock somewhere, then I can put my hand on my heart and say: Yes! In the fall four years ago, I left my bicycle leaning up against this rock and when I came back up from the water's edge to get it, I saw what I have now tried to share with the reader through these few pictures, if only partially.

I don't collect rocks. A person such as myself cannot possibly collect rocks. You can bring home small stones and pebbles in the depths of your pocket, but not rocks. There have been times, when I've been photographing lichen patterns on a plateau or rock face and my companions have asked if I collect pictures of lichen. Then I have to explain that I don't collect anything at all and that you must be very careful with any kind of collecting, since there is so much clutter that accumulates quickly in one's household even without collecting.

Lichens are interesting organisms on the border of the plant and mushroom kingdoms.

 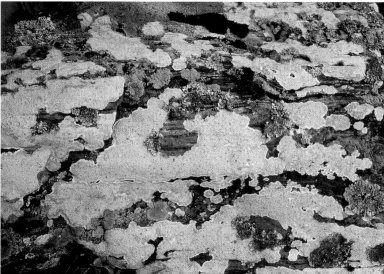

They can be found on trees and planks, on the ground, on rocks and boulders, up in the mountains and in the far north. Lichens are incredibly resilient to harsh climate and yet extremely sensitive to air pollution. Lichens appear before all other life, they are the pioneers. They grow slowly and if left in peace, can live to be very old. I remember listening to a radio show long ago on the subject of Greenland, where the world's oldest live organism had been found on a rock or boulder: a seven or eight hundred year old lichen. Perhaps indeed.

Lichens are beautiful. Lichens are pure. They also have a cleansing effect: you need only look at them up close to feel their harmonizing power. An hour spent in a juniper field by an erratic boulder covered in a cloak of lichen serves as an effective antidote for silly advertising and all other manner of stupidity and spiritual pollution. Such pollution can be found almost anywhere anyone has begun to promote or develop something.

The most amazing colours of lichen are revealed on a cloudy day after the rain. Especially if you look at them with an "enlarging glass", as my mother used to call it.

FALL'S THOUGHTFUL ABSURDITIES

I long for September. I'm waiting for the dark nights and dewy mornings, the flocks of storks, lingonberries and cranberries. I also await the Indian Summer and frosty webs – the sparkle of thousands of threads of spider web in the crisp air of a sunny autumn day. The breeze blows the young spiders Lord know where and Lord knows where from. One flies over the sea, the other ends up right here on a nearby fence post. This is their chance. This is when I enjoy meandering through the forest, collecting mushrooms and taking pictures. This is my chance. Fall fills your soul with peace. I used to hope this was also the case with the autumn of one's life. No such luck.

Also in this anticipation of fall are the colours. What will September bring this time? No two falls are alike. The birches always turn yellow and the bilberry leaves red, but aspen and maple are impossible to predict, as are the rowans at the edge of the field and cloudberry leaves in the bog.

Where does fall get its richness of colour? Nothing happens to the evergreens and mosses, but the leaves… As soon as the days grow shorter, the evacuation of chlorophyll, or the leaf's green begins towards the trunk, allowing the orangey-yellow carotene, bright-yellow xanthophylls and blue, purple and red pigments to emerge in full. Brighter colours in the case of a cold fall, and softer shades if the weather is mild, yet always equally without immediate purpose. Colourful trees and shrubs don't need to tempt insects to fly from one tree to another, or to encourage birds to act in some beneficial way. No responsibility or need, completely voluntary behaviour. So go and look and enjoy! And if, on a gorgeous September afternoon, you glance back at your long string of life experiences, then perhaps in this new light they may appear to you as absurd and pointless – in a thoughtful, fruitful sort of way.

JAPANESE GARDENS
THE ESTONIAN WAY

There is an Estonian saying: years are not brothers. Nor are Estonian autumns all alike, as some people claim. In my memory, one of the most colourful of the last decade was the fall of 1993 and one of its most colourful days, September 23, was spent on Väike-Pakri Island.

"Coastal Swedes" as they were known then, used to live on the Pakri islands. Then came Soviet rule, which blew out the islands' life candle. The villages and churches were turned to ruins and cultivated and arable land was abandoned. The Pakri Islands became an artillery range for planes and all manner of weaponry began to sound there. Although it seems hard to believe, some parts of the Pakri Islands continued to live in utmost peace, because the militarists simply had no business there. Nature took what people had created and continued on as it saw fit: placed junipers and birch to crouch on the feeble meadows, rowans, alder buckthorn and cranberry bush on the thin soil atop the limestone; added some alpine current bushes and mosses for groundcover, with patches of lily of the valley and anemones for good measure. Enchanting scents roam here in the spring, but now, in the fall, the colours dazzle. Something similar can be seen on the crumbled lime surfaces of Osmussaar Island, but in a more subdued palette. It's like a garden, where every square inch has been thoroughly planned and designed, only that no one has planted, trimmed or mowed a thing. Even the paths are traces of times gone by. Wondrous!

A few months following that September day on Väike-Pakri, I was standing in a garden in a small town on the island of Hokkaido and said to my companion: "This is just like in Estonia, on the island of Väike-Pakri". Tadao raised his eyebrows, smiled and said: "But how could it be any other way, Fred?"

A BEAUTIFUL MORNING

"There's frost on the ground," they said earlier, when the grass was covered with hoarfrost at dawn, that made you scrunch up your toes along the outhouse path. Out in the country of course; there are no outhouse paths in the city, nor any hayloft hatches, through which to climb down barefoot onto the frosty morning grass. People from the island of Hiiumaa have their own word for hoarfrost – *huude*. A beautiful Hiiu dialect word, which to my surprise was even known by older people on the Pacific coast, in the Estonian village of Suurekivi as recently as 1978. Summer can bring frosts capable of wilting ferns, but true hoarfrosts are synonymous with fall. Geese fly off and hoarfrosts arrive…

A beautiful hoarfrost morning is not quite an everyday occurrence. A feeble hoarfrost morning – these also come around, as do weepy faces – is not so memorable. A beautiful hoarfrost morning actually begins with a veil of fog the previous evening, which thickens and lasts throughout the entire clear, calm night, so the rays of the rising sun can play games of light in the trees and the cold can go about undisturbed, creating its delicate decorative work amongst the blades of grass, tussocks of stalks and fallen leaves.

Hoarfrost patterns are fine, much finer than those of winter's frost; hoarfrost patterns are sometimes barely visible. These patterns are of course short-lived, as is the case with such beauty. As the sun rises higher and the air warms, the ice crystals melt and dewdrops begin to shine. This is then the continuation of the beautiful hoarfrost morning, accompanied by the young warblers' first experiments of song and the buzzing of wasps and flies.

Sometimes the sounds of geese headed south can be heard in the blue of the sky: bean geese honking, white-fronted geese wailing, as if they were sorry to leave the northland. You can feel the chilly spirit of fall in the air.

THE SEA IS RAGING

The sea is raging. So this was what the daylong stillness foretold: the calm before the storm.

I've spent a few years living on the island of Hiiumaa, but made it to the Ristna tip of the Kōpu peninsula only after the guard towers, barriers and barbed wire were gone. I'm witnessing a north-western storm here for the first time.

It's an impressive sight. Since for some reason the waves always come ashore at a right angle, a cross-wave pattern develops at this skinny spit of land, which in a storm becomes a churning mass of water. You stand on a bank of small rocks and stare bewitched at nature's rage beneath the grey October sky. Occasionally the sun breaks through a rift in the clouds and for a moment lights up the surface of the sea. If this happens during bouts of rain, then a rainbow appears above the foamy surf, like a vision from the powers of the skies.

It's a joy to watch this from the shore, especially if you can run into an old bunker for shelter from the nastier bouts of weather, but I wouldn't like to end up in such a rage in a sailboat or life raft. You are but a speck of dust in this world full of the unexpected and you know very well that it's not possible to live beyond the supreme laws, but there's a desire in your blood nonetheless. The desire to have even the smallest imaginable piece of land beneath your feet, to have a guarantee and feeling of security – so that the apparent peace does not create unease.

When your blood begins to rage, there is nothing more to count on. Then there's no surface, on which to rest your feet, no bunker into which to flee; no sense of security or any guarantee.

This battle of primal powers is horrific, whether it be on the sea, or in your veins, yet it is exciting, arousing and beautiful as well. You stand enraptured before it, for you are powerless against nature's fundamental spirit. It can toss your ship to pieces, but it also cleans shore. And there is no doubt that peace will come again, since at one time storms also ravaged the shores of Ristna where a pine forest now roars in the wind.

LIVE DEAD TREES

I had actually thought about bringing you to visit these old trees in the summer, but why should October be a less suitable time for this little hike than July? The old, silent pine doesn't care after all, when people come by it, stop, knock on its echoing trunk, look at what was once a majestic crown, roaring in the sea wind, walk around it, perhaps take a picture, or simply look at it and go on their way. Just like for some people, visiting a certain tomb or tombstone may be a greater event than all of the meetings with live people in the past week, some people fondly remember dead tree giants in the middle of a live forest in the same way.

To this day, a dead pine stands in the Kõrvemaa region by Kreo Kalajärv – Kreo Fish Lake, from which I saw my first osprey take off fifty-two years ago. The osprey is long gone from the Kreo Lakes and not even a memory remains of its nesting tree of long ago, but its lookout tree still stands. I know that it does, because every time I happen to be in the area, I go check, to see if it is. And when I travel in Hiiumaa, or in the forests of Alutaguse or Nõva, where I know the bearded tree skeletons standing on the edge of a bog or on dunes, then I detour onto trails that lead to them, to see how they're holding up; whether a raven or bird of prey has perhaps lost a feather beneath them, or left a white mark. Some of these large old trees have decayed and fallen over the decades and are growing moss on their trunks, but mostly they are still standing and provide shelter to a good many beings. I now know that they will outlive me and this knowledge fills my spirit with a special kind of peace. This no doubt because we're surrounded by so much senseless loss and tragedy.

REDPOLL

Imagine a gaggle of guests arriving at your door at the most inappropriate time and joyfully announcing "We're here and we're staying for quite a while!" Redpolls never arrive in this way. The redpolls arrival from the north is forecast long in advance and that's why it hasn't happened, that they have eaten us bare of birch, alder or grass seed.

It's always exciting when awaited guests such as these begin to arrive: tiny and peaceful, who get along famously with each other, never fight and are beautiful to boot. Redpolls are a bit like siskins, but slightly larger and greyish-brown (greenish-yellow dominates in the siskin's plumage), with a crimson-red forehead and whitish belly; males are identifiable by their pinkish breast. During the winter, when some of those who have remained behind appear on a birdfeeder, you can clearly see their plumage in all its glory. Since redpolls have no real fear of humans, it's sometimes possible to study them up-close on bare birch branches or balancing on alder catkins. (Its Estonian name *urvalind* means catkin bird.) They can be spotted beginning in mid-September, but more often in October-November. The accompanying photo of a redpoll was taken from a distance of a few metres on an overcast October day long ago on the island of Hiiumaa. They journey south for the winter, some to central Europe, some south-east and east. Redpolls tagged in Finland have even reached Altai.

The redpoll's song can be heard in the spring, in March and April, when they pass through on their travels northward in restless flocks numbering in the hundreds. It can also be heard when we chance upon nesting birds while travelling in the tundra in June. It has been speculated that redpolls also nest in Estonia, but this has remained as speculation. For us, redpolls are winter birds. Redpolls are guests and as awaited guests they deserve to be recalled with fondness and a good word.

FALL IN WINTER

Leaves rain down upon the snow. Usually the leaves fall first and then the snow, but this time the opposite was true: the leaves were still clinging to the trees and it snowed. Not just a few flakes, but a good solid blanket of white, lasting an entire week. Well, what do you know! People out in the park stop to admire the leaves, children buzz about excitedly and photographers capture the scene. Gorgeous! And it just keeps getting better, as more leaves trickle down from the trees – yellow, red, brown and many more paler shades – all onto the clean white canvas. This didn't happen before! What could it possibly mean?

Long ago, in the historic days of my youth, I sent a girl a picture of a mushroom in the guise of a postcard. Someone had left their developed film out to dry in the lab. I looked at them, and finding some to be extremely interesting, I enlarged two or three of them on the sly. I glued a stamp behind one of them, wrote the girl's name and address, a little something to the girl as well and popped it the mail. Oh, the confusion that followed! What do the mushrooms mean? *Mother, what can Fred possibly mean sending me mushrooms? What is he trying to say?* Her female classmates had also grown excited – the boy's gone nuts while off at Tartu University, sending girls pictures of mushrooms. There's got to be another angle here…

Naturally it has to mean something. That's always the case if something is suddenly contrary to the usual. Confusion. Excitement at least.

So what's the big deal about a boy's photos of a mushroom, or snow in October, but it certainly is memorable. It's unexpected, it's different, uncommon. I recall another time, a dozen or so years ago, when I emerged from my cabin after an early snowfall to check out the weather. It was actually the previous day's snow and now the willows were covering it with colourful sprinkles. The sky hung grey and low and the snow was patterned with coloured leaves. And what colours they were! It is said that life is never completely black or white. But if the adventures and events of our lives were to be placed on an appropriate backdrop, then black and white would no doubt emphasize their meaning and various shades most effectively.

Autumn leaves on an inky black pond is quite a common sight, but they're much rarer on freshly fallen snow. Perhaps that's why black seems more predictable and familiar and white so surprising, yet both are definitely demanding.

THE HOARFROSTS ARE COMING

Hoarfrosts arrive silently, at night, they come as if stalking. You step outside in the morning and discover a layer of frost covering the ground. In the days of old, when folk sayings were not taken lightly, this was preceded by rows of geese honking in the sky, but now you can no longer be sure of such things, since times are changing. But still, the grass and fallen leaves beneath trees are often frost-covered in the month of November.

As a boy I didn't really like November. There was not much daylight-time left over after school, in the morning you had to practically feel your way to school in the dark and the evenings became pitch-dark in no time. Sundays also tended to often be dusky and non-descript. Some relief was provided in the form of the first skateable ice on smaller ponds and hikes onto the frozen plowed land beyond the city, where hares jumped up and fled towards the woods. But one sound has remained in my memory since then.

It just so happened, that around the time of the former Soviet November holidays, we were able to get away to some far-off lakes in the forest. There I broke away pieces of translucent ice with the heel of my boot and threw them onto the lake with great force. They fell to pieces and made the lake ring out and that incredible shattering sound echoed back from the forest like a screaming loud protest in reaction to this most horrid offence against nature in its time of deepest peace. The forest and lake had long prepared for this peace and then suddenly someone comes along and defaces it in a brutal manner. I can hear those shatterings of long ago inside me even now, when some unexpected adventure or unforeseen event breaks into the peace of my life's autumnal hoarfrost mornings, like a little boy keen on finding entertainment.

Sometimes this can be quite miraculous, but there are times when miraculous things can also cause pain.

PERAKÜLA NOVEMBER

November yet again, well what are you going to do? I overhear women, for some reason women and not men saying: "Once again this dreary, dark time". Perhaps men are simply not able to understand dreary and dark and they don't care, as is also the case with many beautiful and fair things in this world. Is it really that bad?

While I was in school, I didn't ponder over such things, for that was the time to go to school. Later, when I started working, I occasionally felt that late fall is indeed a dreary time, but later still, the dusk began to show itself in a different light, sometimes downright brightly. Now I look at the bare trees and traces of snow on the ground and I wonder what is so special about the November light.

I spent a week in Peraküla one November a few years back. Not everyone may know where Peraküla is. Peraküla is in north-eastern Estonia, near Nõva. A lot of people have now started visiting the area in the summer, but during the Soviet era, no one knew much more about Peraküla, other than that it was part of the forbidden border zone. Peraküla is groves of heath pines that smell of resin and ozone, tiny lakes amidst forests and the rush of waves on the sandy seashore. Peraküla is dark red helleborine along the roadsides in summer and the purple of heather as far as the eye can see and Peraküla is also a lot of blueberries, lingonberries and porcini mushrooms. But Peraküla in November is peace and quiet. During that memorable week, I walked to the seashore and forest every day. These weren't long, since walks are never long. These walks were not for the sake of observation or pondering important thoughts.

I wandered these same paths over and over again, without meeting a soul, accompanied by the whispering of the pines and sounds of the sea. The paths led nowhere, I only saw my own footprints in the freshly fallen snow on the next day, the one after that and the next day after that, and this only served to prove that I had already wandered there before. Following the commotion of huge cities and chaotic airports, after days of speeding along highways and the heavy, taxing flow of shifting kaleidoscopic impressions from far-off lands, I sometimes wonder whether it will ever be possible to spend a eternally brief November week wandering as I please, following my own footprints along Peraküla's forest paths, bogs and coastal sands. Perhaps it is? One day, perhaps.

PATTERNS IN MY WALLS

The tree's ring marks cannot be seen from a distance, only the ends of the logs in the wall. In the walls of a cabin, the walls of a shed, the walls of a barn, the walls of a sauna, all nicely corner to corner. You step closer and begin to see more; look really closely and see stories. Some stories are simple and straightforward from the start: a happy childhood amongst your own kind on a comfy hillock somewhere, then some better and some worse times like always, and so on, until the beginning of a new life in the wall of a building. There are also stories of very different fates close by. You could assume that they're not all that different, since most likely these logs have been cut at the same time in the same forest, yet something did happen. A hare nibbled a young tree. A stag rubbed his antlers. A bear scratched. Someone swung an axe. A grenade exploded in the forest.

I was nine years old when we were hit by the hail of bombs in Tallinn. The knots created on that horrific night will never fade from within my life pattern. But the next morning we were alive, all of the people in our house, and in a few days the children were sent out of harms way to Viljandimaa county. Nothing will serve to shadow the unforgettable spring and summer of 1944 at the Loodi orphanage. It was the birth of the harmony of the world, regardless of the fact that we were covered in lice and suffered from countless stomach ailments. Lice couldn't put a damper on the summer smells of Mulgimaa and the beauty of its landscapes. Other minor problems came and went. Or didn't. One boy died. The boy's mother took care of us, when we were ill. I remember her eyes, red from crying. They left a mark within me, of which I'm reminded when my thoughts wander along those paths. And then continuing on with new times and different adventures and events and – new patterns. Years are not similar, like brothers.

You live, and the forest of humans around you rustles, full of mysterious ferns and child-like flowers of the wood. People like trees. Some stand with dignity and confidence, some rub against others, squeaking when the slightest wind arises. Some snap in a storm, some rot while standing, some fall for others to carry; for what can you do, if your roots begin to fail and the ground is poor? Some, God bless, have rot in the crown, like a man from the island of Saaremaa said about his crazy neighbour. But when the saw-man reaches the forest, everything changes. And the saw-man will arrive and with him the loss. After the saw-man there will be no forest or stories, for how many trees can fit in a wall to later tell their mute stories to those viewing them close up? How many people are there, who are interested in the stories of others? Never mind the fact that others' stories are actually patterns in my wall.

NORTHERN LIGHTS

Late one night, long ago, we awoke to hear mother calling: "Boys, come quick, the sky is full of northern lights!" This must've been before the war, because I remember the city lights glowing. Since the northern sky was not well visible from our living room window, we grabbed some coats and went out onto the street in front of the house, where the entire sky opened up to us. Others from our building were already outside and people had also gathered in front of neighbouring houses. I recall the brightness and silence of the night and gasps of women bundled up in coats. But most of all I remember the bewitching light of those "merry sky dancers", which seemed to wane at times, only to explode with brilliant rays and renewed energy. The city lights didn't bother us, since they were hidden behind the railway embankment.

The silent majesty of this festive yet chilling scene held me in its grasp. Why this strange light so suddenly, why now, in the northern sky? No one could give us any sensible explanation, we were simply told "Those, boys, are northern lights, take it all in and when you've had enough, go back to bed." We didn't get enough, but had no choice but to crawl back into bed. I so wanted to discuss the lights with my brother, but what was there to say? There they were, the northern lights, shining mysteriously through the crocheted lace curtains into my room.

That night long ago gave me a most specific recognition of earthliness and godliness. That there is the earthly realm but yet there is more, which is not quite heavenly, yet somehow arches over, in a way untouched by early things, without might or power, fear or love and you can think or believe what you will. Sometimes this something appears and not a soul can predict the night and manner in which it will occur, but if you wish to discuss it later then you can't, because you don't know how, since you have no words and you know why there are no words and what it is, for which there are no words. Then it's as though a voice calls: *Aurora borealis* and that is all the wisdom at your disposal, with which you must now ponder the nature and purpose of all that arches above your earthly being.

OLD RED

I found myself in southern Estonia for the first time at the beginning of the second half of the last century. When compared to Lasnamäe's barren limestone plateau and the low forests around Tallinn, it left quite an impression. I was nineteen years old at the time. I had seen some pictures of Pühajärv Lake in books and knew of Taevaskoda, a famous sandstone denudation, only through stories. We visited Pühajärv, or Holy Lake, with our class while on a cycling trip one beautiful June evening. I visited Taevaskoda a few months later with my friend from Tartu and continued going there for the next five years. Getting there by train from Tartu was easy and the university had a biology research station at Taevaskoda, where we dried plants collected for our herbarium and tallied up our water skimmers and other small creatures caught in the Ahja River. We saw emerald-green kingfishers flying along the river in summer and dippers keeping watch on the rocks amongst the rapids in winter. There was the hollow calling of the tawny owl on a spring evening and bats above the water, oh how many bats on summer nights! There was the Maiden's Cave, the Mother Spring, moonlight and the kind of stories to which my world-wise aunt would say: "Better to believe it, than not". Ülo – he was the one who took me to Taevaskoda for the first time – told me, that if you drink from the Mother's Spring with a girl on the night of a full moon, then love will blossom. Ülo told a lot of stories, but I remembered the drinking in the moonlight story and am glad I did, because I was thereby able to avoid many a misunderstanding.

Ülo's visits to the Mother Spring with girls were well known, during the full moon I mean. And it was obvious that it was an enchanted spring and I couldn't understand why Ülo didn't understand that any manner of sorcery is not to be taken lightly, not even if you've made it up yourself. I'm not aware of Ülo having gone to the spring at Taevaskoda in his later years, but the man remained insatiable until the end of his days.

Indeed, Taevaskoda's cliffs are truly beautiful. If the red sandstone rock face of Greater Taevaskoda rises to a height of 22 metres, then approximately four hundred and fifty metres of these Devonian sediments stretch down beneath the ground.

Why are the Taevaskoda cliffs red? This is explained in a straightforward manner on page 60 of the nature volume of the series "Eesti", published in 1995: "The sediments' red colour is due to a layer of iron hydroxides created at the time when certain colloids were sifted out, usually immediately following their formation. Red-coloured, cross-layered sandstones are arid climate sediments, known internationally as Old Red formations." It's easier to not ponder over when these mystifying events took place: 405-350 million years ago…

The last time I wandered about the silent Taevaskoda forests was a couple of years back in the fall. The cliffs are now fifty years older, but still just as red. We all come and go, but you Old Red, remain.

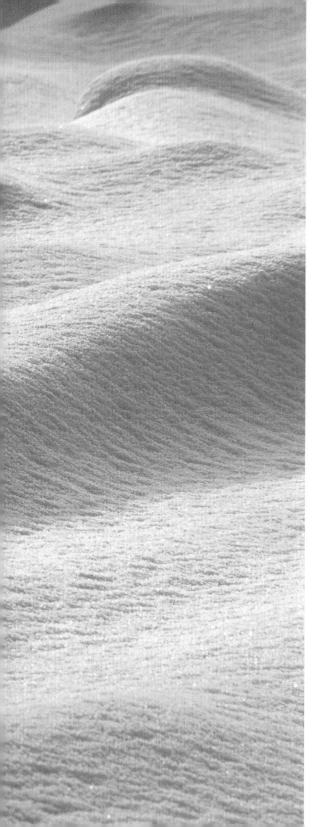

SNOW

The snow came down and the river turned to ice. There is a lot to ponder when fall "runs out" and winter literally "arrives in your hand" as per direct translation. This said in an endlessly beautiful language, which allows movement of that which is natural and divine, although such everyday phenomena can also be said in other ways.

Yes, but about the snow…

If you haven't ever seen snow before, then it's striking. Snow surprises with the simple fact of how it falls. I was three years old, when I saw my first snow after the tropical rains. In the summer, people said that snow falls from the sky like rainwater, but is white, soft and cold, and falls to the ground slowly. I stared at the white clouds in the August sky and saw in my mind's eye how one day that cotton batten would start sinking down from the sky in chunks the size of pillows. Exactly how, and just how much of the mysterious white stuff there is, no one knows. Look and ask as much as you want, you will only see that big people simply do not understand your questions. The answer is always one and the same: "Wait, you'll see one day".

There have been few days that I have waited for as much, perhaps no other, like that one promised day. I remember that mother was at the kitchen table, whizzing with the sewing machine and I was on the floor in front of the stove, in the midst of some kind game when an important message arrived: "Come look, it's snowing!" I climbed onto a chair by the window and looked outside. It was snowing. The boys next door, who had been playing ball in the meadow by the railway dam, lightly-clothed, raced inside and the weather suddenly seemed greyer than ever before, only it was a totally different kind of grey. Yes, it was snowing, with a wind; thick white snow. To this day, I'm not able to say anything more about the indescribable scene that opened up to me through the kitchen window that day.

There was a lot of snow that winter long ago. Clean, white, soft snow in which I could trek about, plow through on tiny skis smelling of wood tar and steer a Finnish push-sledge with my brother. I pick it up in my hand – it melts. Not like butter in a pan or sugar in your mouth, but in a way that snow only melts in a child's hand or under his or her collar. A snowball fight is the most innocent fight, a snowman the mutest man. Without snow there would be no snow shovels or ski marathons and no white rabbits would live in the woods, not to mention the amazing winter light.

Countless numbers of people under the sun never see snow or know anything about winter. How on earth can they live like that?! Perhaps since there are others elsewhere, who live their entire lives amid fields of snow and ice. Or maybe because some lucky person somewhere is able to press his hot face into the soft snow and listen to how footsteps squeak on a hard-packed path in the frigid cold.

WINTERY TIT

The tit flies to my windowsill:
belly yellow, white under cheek;
pecks away, pecks away, peers knowingly
inside – that's the tit's way –,
belly yellow, white under cheek!

Juhan Liiv

Winter arrives and tits (or chickadees, as they are called in North America) begin to arrive in the yard and come to the window. They come alone, in pairs and in large groups. Great tits and blue tits, marsh tits, occasionally a lone coal tit, but not long-tailed tits; they prefer to roam the forests, as do crested tits, who live only on the mainland. One of the most prominent members of this already colourful bunch is of course the great tit, the most numerous and ambitious of the clan. They're the ones that tap on your window in the morning and peer inside, tug the tow fibre from cracks in the wall, and rip the wallpaper in an abandoned house, if they manage to get inside through a broken window. The great tit makes everything its business; it has the heart of a discoverer and the spirit of an adventurer. The distance that a chaffinch travels during 4 hours of migration, takes the tit an entire day. A tit in dire straits becomes a courageous fighter, who admits no defeat. When it finds itself in a bird bander's trap, the great tit begins to frantically search for a weak spot. If it thinks it's found it, a feverish filing of the bars ensues. Since the bars won't give, a new spot is quickly found and all of this activity is accompanied by an angry chattering. And when the "hairy hand" finally nabs the bird, the battle continues, and lasts until the bander finally opens up his or her palm. Even then, the enraged black beak can sometimes not bear to release its grip.

A wintery tit most certainly wishes to eat, be it a spring chicken or ruler of the roost. It longs for fat and suet, sunflower seeds and rolled oats, it yearns for them from dawn 'til dusk, one beakful at a time and not by gobbling for later, in the manner of jays. They want to live, as do we all. This is what the winter tit desires and it wouldn't hurt, if this need not require much effort, and if it really doesn't, then why not take some snacks from an outstretched hand? It's such a funny and an odd, exhilarating feeling, when a tit perches on your finger to grab a morsel from your palm. Such a wonderful feeling and not the kind of feeling as when a person shows their readiness to eat from the palm of your hand and thinks that you'll enjoy it too.

Welcome wintery tit and may the winter have mercy on all of us.